W9-ABQ-355

A Day in the Life: Rain Forest Animals

Poison Dart Frog

Anita Ganeri

Heinemann Library
Chicago, IL

www.heinemannraintree.com
Visit our website to find out more information about Heinemann-Raintree books.

To order:
☎ Phone 888-454-2279
🖥 Visit www.heinemannraintree.com to browse our catalog and order online.

Edited by Nancy Dickmann, Rebecca Rissman, and Catherine Veitch
Designed by Steve Mead
Picture research by Mica Brancic
Originated by Capstone Global Library
Printed and bound in China by South China Printing Company Ltd

14 13 12 11 10
10 9 8 7 6 5 4 3 2 1

Library of Congress Cataloging-in-Publication Data
Ganeri, Anita, 1961-
  Poison dart frog / Anita Ganeri.
     p. cm.—(A day in the life. Rain forest animals)
  Includes bibliographical references and index.
  ISBN 978-1-4329-4104-8 (hc)—ISBN 978-1-4329-4115-4 (pb) 1. Dendrobatidae—Juvenile literature. I. Title.
  QL668.E233G36 2011
  597.87'7—dc22
                                    2010000959

Acknowledgments
We would like to thank the following for permission to reproduce photographs: Corbis pp. 15, 18(© Michael & Patricia Fogden), 22 (© Paul Souders); FLPA pp. 9, 10, 19, 23 tadpole (Minden Pictures/Thomas Marent), 14, 17, 20, 23 blow dart (Minden Pictures/Mark Moffett), 16 (Minden Pictures/Albert Lleal); Nature Picture Library p. 13 (© Tim Laman); Photolibrary pp. 4 (age fotostock/Peter Lilja), 6, 23 poisonous (age fotostock/Andoni Canela), 7 (Fotosearch), 11 (Oxford Scientific (OSF)/Brian Kenney), 12, 23 prey (Mauritius/Rauschenbach Rauschenbach), 21 (Design Pics Inc/Corey Hochachka); Shutterstock pp. 5, 23 amphibian (Pavel Mikoska), 23 rain forest (© Szefei).

Cover photograph of poison dart frog on moss reproduced with permission of Corbis (© Joe McDonald).

Back cover photographs of (left) a poison dart frog's tongue reproduced with permission of Photolibrary (Mauritius/Rauschenbach Rauschenbach); and (right) a poison dart tadpole reproduced with permission of Corbis (© Michael & Patricia Fogden).

We would like to thank Michael Bright for his invaluable help in the preparation of this book.

Every effort has been made to contact copyright holders of material reproduced in this book. Any omissions will be rectified in subsequent printings if notice is given to the publisher.

All the Internet addresses (URLs) given in this book were valid at the time of going to press. However, due to the dynamic nature of the Internet, some addresses may have changed, or sites may have changed or ceased to exist since publication. While the author and publisher regret any inconvenience this may cause readers, no responsibility for any such changes can be accepted by either the author or the publisher.

Contents

Some words are in bold, **like this**. You can find them in the glossary on page 23.

What Are Poison Dart Frogs?

Poison dart frogs are tiny frogs.

There are many different types of poison dart frogs.

toad

Poison dart frogs belong to a group of animals known as **amphibians**.

Toads, newts, and salamanders are also amphibians.

What Do Poison Dart Frogs Look Like?

Poison dart frogs can be yellow, blue, green, red, black, or orange.

Their brightly colored skin is **poisonous**.

The bright colors make the frogs easy for birds and other animals to see.

The colors warn other animals that the frogs are not good to eat.

Where Do Poison Dart Frogs Live?

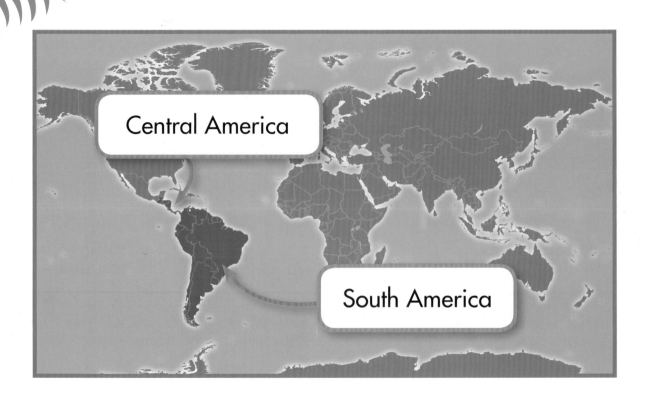

Central America

South America

Poison dart frogs live in the **rain forests** of Central America and South America.

It is warm and wet in the rain forest all year long.

Most poison dart frogs live on the forest floor.

They take shelter under rocks and plants close to small streams or pools.

What Do the Frogs Do During the Day?

Poison dart frogs are very active during the day.

They search for food on the forest floor and take care of their young.

Some poison dart frogs live in small groups.

Others live in pairs made up of one male and one female.

What Do Poison Dart Frogs Eat?

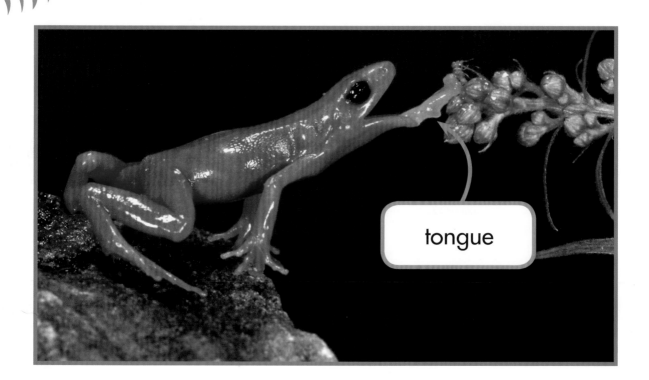

tongue

A poison dart frog eats tiny insects and spiders.

It grabs its **prey** with its long, sticky tongue and pulls it into its mouth.

insect

Poison dart frogs get their poison from the insects they eat.

The insects get their poison from the plants they feed on.

Does Anything Hunt Poison Dart Frogs?

blow dart

Some people catch poison dart frogs.

They use the poison from the frogs on **blow darts** to kill animals for food.

poison dart frog

Most **rain forest** animals leave poison dart frogs alone.

But the fire-bellied snake likes eating the frogs and is not hurt by their poison.

Where Are the Baby Frogs Born?

eggs

Some poison dart frogs lay their eggs on the forest floor.

Other poison dart frogs lay their eggs on leaves.

eggs

The eggs are covered in jelly to stop them from drying out.

The parents guard the eggs for about two weeks until they hatch into tiny **tadpoles**.

Do Poison Dart Frogs Take Care of their Young?

tadpole

Poison dart frogs are caring parents.

When their **tadpoles** hatch, the parents carry them to water where they can grow into frogs.

The water may be a small pond or a pool of rainwater inside a leaf.

The parents feed the tadpoles plants, young insects, and eggs that did not hatch.

What Do the Frogs Do at Night?

At night, poison dart frogs do not go to sleep in the same way that you do.

Instead, they sit very still and rest.

Some poison dart frogs like to rest under piles of leaves on the forest floor.

Other frogs rest in small holes in the ground.

Poison Dart Frog Body Map

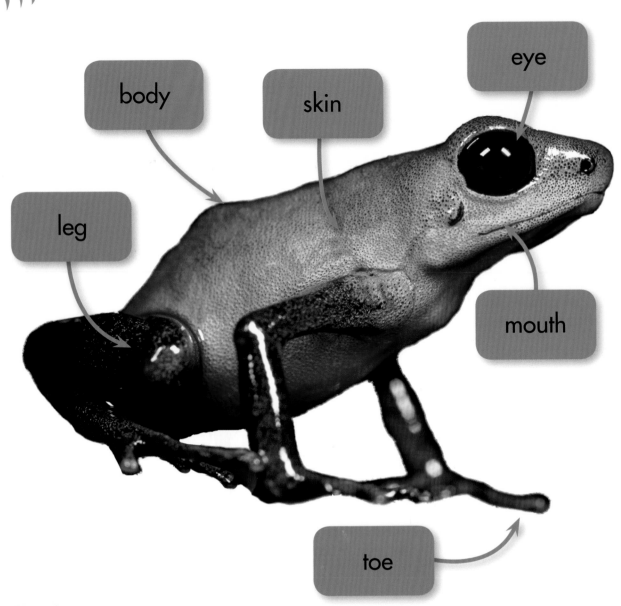

body

skin

eye

leg

mouth

toe

Glossary

amphibian animal that lives partly on water and partly on land

blow dart pointed dart used for hunting

poisonous may cause illness or death

prey animal that is hunted by other animals for food

rain forest thick forest with very tall trees and a lot of rain

tadpole young frog

Find Out More

Books

Bredeson, Carmen. *Poison Dart Frogs Up Close.* Berkeley Heights, NJ: Enslow Elementary, 2009.

Dussling, Jennifer. *Deadly Poison Dart Frogs.* New York, NY: Bearport, 2009.

Websites

www.sandiegozoo.org/animalbytes/t-poison_frog.html

http://nationalzoo.si.edu/Animals/Amazonia/Facts/fact-poisondartfrog.cfm

http://kids.nationalgeographic.com/Animals/CreatureFeature/Poison-dart-frog

Index